CAPE COD

THE OLD WINDMILL (1793)—EASTHAM

CAPE COD

A PHOTOGRAPHIC
SKETCHBOOK

SANDWICH

BY

Samuel Chamberlain

HASTINGS HOUSE, PUBLISHERS
NEW YORK

Brewster

Yarmouthport

FOREWORD

CAPE COD means many things to many people. To some fortunate families it signifies a summer's tranquility, a mild and caressing climate, and a civilized retreat from the cacaphony and strain of the city. For them this is an enchanted refuge where they may enjoy their own comfortable, shingle-clad house. It is the setting for a daily game of golf, a dip along a sandy beach and a wonderful place where their children grow up year after year with the same summer friends.

The casual visitor has a less domestic impression of Cape Cod, but a more exciting one. To his eyes everything is novel and unforeseen and fascinating. He has never gazed upon a cranberry bog before, nor upon such a profusion of roses in June. The novelty of lighthouses and windmills centuries old, of sand dunes and salt marshes, intrigues him. Cotuit oysters, beach plum jelly, Sandwich glass, and the summer theatre as it flourishes in Dennis, are new and refreshing. To this receptive visitor the Cape is a hospitable haven, studded with comfortable country hotels and with pitch-roofed cottages along the shore, each claiming its own private stretch of sandy beach. The siren call of this particular Cape Cod is heard softly throughout the land and the response comes from every state in the Union, as a study of visiting license plates will prove.

There is another facet of this sandy promontory, one which is more closely associated with Portugese fishermen, Indian cranberry pickers, Yankee storekeepers and retired Wall Streeters. These are the authentic, year-'round residents, and they know the Cape's darker moods as well as its summer smiles. They know the contrast between a June morning on the village green in Falmouth and a storm on the bluffs of Truro in winter, bitten by savage Atlantic winds. Yet something about the majesty and solitude of these far reaches has attracted American writers for generations, and they are perhaps the best known of the Cape's full-time citizens.

At the turn of the century an art school was established in Provincetown, an innovation which has led far, for Cape Cod has now become the country's outstanding summer art colony. Painters, etchers and water colorists have recorded its multiple charms since that day, and Cape Cod landscapes have stood out in big city art exhibitions for just as long. Photographers have also had their fling on the Cape. The startling contrast of dune, sky and sea makes it peculiarly photogenic. A lighthouse or a windblown pine has always aroused a creative urge in a cameraman. There are other, subtler subjects to challenge him — pathways lined with boxwood, fresh water ponds, village churches and abandoned fishing boats lying idle in the sands. The Cape Cod cottage, so widely adapted to solve today's housing problem, offers him a dozen quaint variations. But the photographer has his troubles too, principally with telephone poles, roadside signs, television antennae, and other unlovely externals of this brash mid-century. But the beauty of the Cape is still there, and this despite the ravages of two comparatively recent hurricanes.

This book sets out to capture some of that beauty by means of the photographic image. The wandering camera sketches, in these pages, a progressive portrait of Cape Cod, beginning as soon as it crosses the Canal on a bright spring morning and ending with an autumn sunset in Provincetown. Between these extremes it advances through the Cape's fifteen towns and scores of villages, seeking to record the picturesqueness, the subtlety, and the warmth of this benign hook of land in seventy-three snaps of the shutter. This is a large order, and in such a limited space one can only hope to catch an *impression* of this ancient and fascinating peninsula, the first landing place of the Pilgrim fathers, and the favorite summer retreat of thousands of their descendants. If only a fragment of Cape Cod's indefinable charm has thus been captured, the shutter will not, as goes the time-worn phrase, have clicked in vain.

SAMUEL CHAMBERLAIN

7 TWO BRIDGES OVER CAPE COD CANAL   *Bourne*

THE INLET

Monument Beach

9 APTUXCET TRADING POST   *Bourne*

JUNE MORNING

Pocasset
10

THE CLASSIC CAPE COD COTTAGE   *Sandwich*

THE DILLINGHAM HOUSE (1650)   *Sandwich*

BASIC CAPE COD ARCHITECTURE   *Sandwich*

THE BROOK

East Sandwich

THE GREEN   *Falmouth*

THE HISTORICAL SOCIETY (1790)   *Falmouth*

FISH PIER   *Woods Hole*

17

NOBSKA POINT LIGHT

Falmouth

18

FRESH WATER FLOWS INTO BUZZARD'S BAY   *Old Silver Beach*

LITTLE WHITE CHURCH

Waquoit

THE FARM

Mashpee

DOMESTICATED WINDMILL

Oyster Harbors

SILVER SHORE   *Craigville Beach*

PLEASURE CRAFT

Osterville

ROWBOAT REFUGE   *Hyannis*

THE OLD CROCKER TAVERN (1754)   *Barnstable*

THE BIRCHES

Cummaquid

THE MARSHES

Yarmouthport

28

CAPE SCALLOPS

Yarmouthport

STATELY BACKYARD OF THE THACHER HOUSE   *Yarmouth*

OLD YARMOUTH INN   *Yarmouth*

LATE AFTERNOON

Bass River

SCREEN OF SAPLINGS   *Yarmouthport*

NOONTIME SHADOWS

Dennis

THE PITCH-ROOFED COTTAGE *Dennis*

EARLY AUTUMN

South Yarmouth

36

SENILE SENTINELS

West Dennis

37

GREEK REVIVAL CHURCH

FISHERMEN'S INLET

Harwichport

THE OLD MILL

41 LOBSTER POT PANORAMA *Chatham*

DOORWAY OF THE OLD ATWOOD HOUSE (1752)   *Chatham*

42

CHATHAM LIGHT

THE GRACEFUL WAY OF LIFE

COLLECTION OF LOBSTER BUOYS   *Chatham*

45

SILVER SEEDLINGS   *Brewster*
46

THE FLAGSTONE PATH

South Orleans

MEETING HOUSE

East Orleans
48

THE BLUE ATLANTIC

Orleans Beach

MILL POND AT NAUSET HEIGHTS

Orleans

COUNTRY STORE

Orleans

EARLY CAPE COD COTTAGE (1730) *Eastham*

INLAND WATERWAY   *Eastham*

OLD MEETING HOUSE IN SPRING *Wellfleet*

JULY HIGH NOON

Wellfleet

HIGH AND DRY   *Wellfleet*

FLOWERY HILLSIDE   *Wellfleet*

AGING BRANCHES

THE DUNES *Truro*

HIGHLAND LIGHT

Truro

FALLEN VETERAN   *Truro*

STILL WATERS AT POND VILLAGE

Truro

SIDE STREET—EARLY SPRING   *Provincetown*

PROVINCETOWN ACROSS THE BAY

Truro

FISH PIER AT SUNSET   *Provincetown*

POLE WHARF

Provincetown

LOW TIDE   *Provincetown*

THE OLDEST HOUSE IN PROVINCETOWN

ARTIST'S MODEL

Provincetown

SKELETON IN THE SAND   *Race Point*

AUTUMN'S LAST FLICKER   *Pilgrim Lake*